ANIMALS IN THE WILD

SIBERIAN TIGER

Annette Whipple

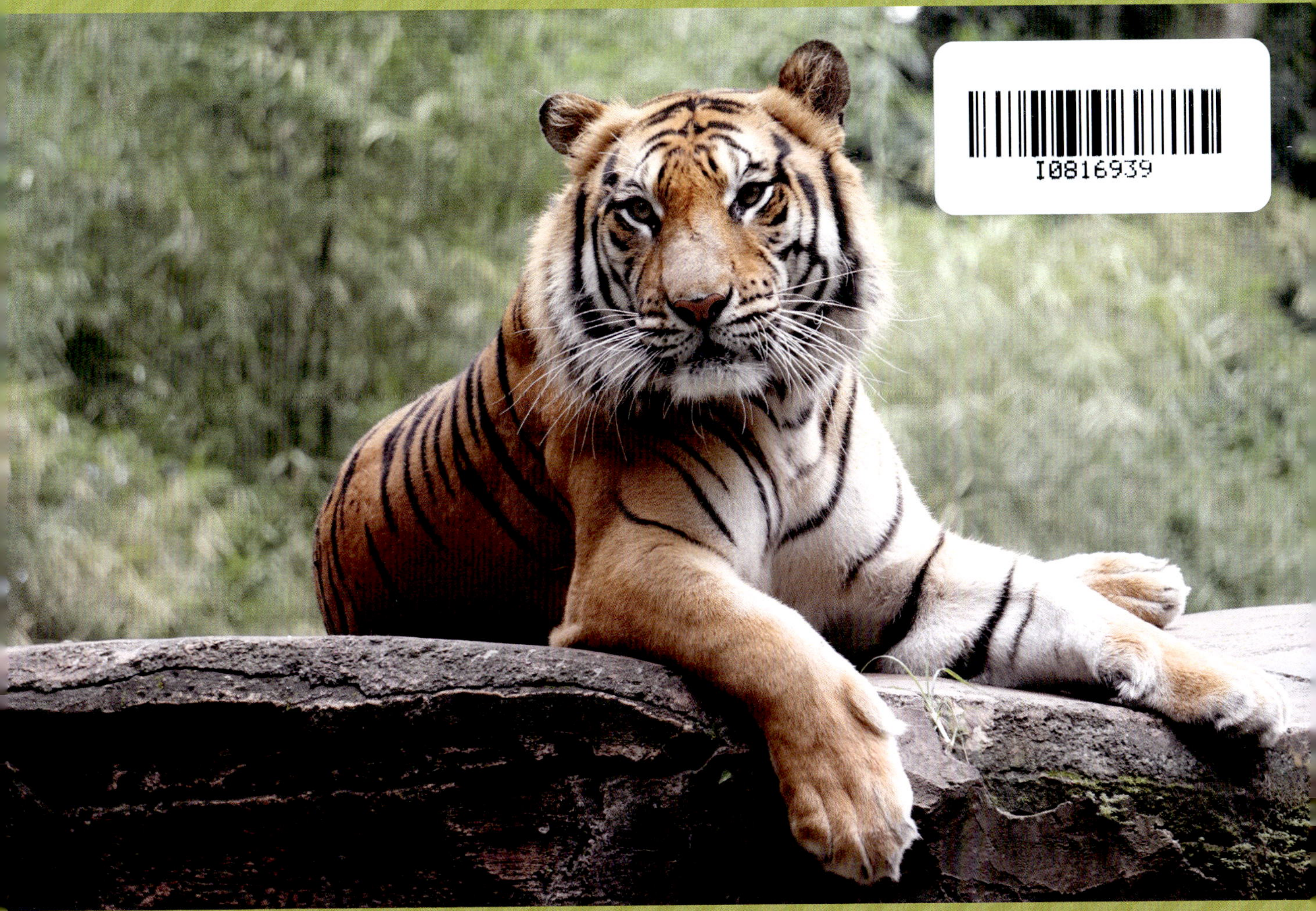

A Crabtree Forest Book

Notes for Readers and Class Discussion

This book is designed to teach readers about core subject areas, build curiosity, and inspire further investigation. Readers are encouraged to build upon what they already know about the subject and engage in topics they want to learn more about. Here are a few guiding questions to prompt reflection and discussion. Possible answers appear in red.

Before Reading:

Read the title and look at the table of contents. What do you already know about Siberian tigers?

- *I know that Siberian tigers live in very cold regions of the world.*
- *I know that Siberian tigers are carnivores.*

What would you like to learn about Siberian tigers?

- *I would like to learn about how the Siberian tiger hunts its prey.*
- *I would like to learn whether the Siberian tiger is endangered.*

During Reading:

Pause after reading each page or chapter. What questions do you have about what you read? What are you curious to know?

- *I wonder why Siberian tigers hunt their prey at night.*
- *I am curious to know why many Siberian tigers live in captivity.*

Make connections to what you are reading. How is this like something you already know?

- *I know that animals have adaptations that allow them to live in extreme environments, such as freezing cold.*
- *I know that one of the biggest threats to animals in the wild is habitat loss due to human actions, such as deforestation.*

After Reading:

Recall key details about the book. What was the author trying to teach readers?

- *The author was trying to teach readers about the characteristics, behaviors, and habitats of Siberian tigers.*
- *The author was trying to teach readers that Siberian tigers are an endangered species and at risk of becoming extinct if they are not protected.*

How did the images and captions help you understand more?

- *The photographs helped to show me how a Siberian tiger lives and hunts.*
- *The captions helped me understand new details about Siberian tigers.*

Table of Contents

Meet the Siberian Tiger

What **feline** is the largest of all the cats in the world? The Siberian tiger! This enormous big cat is native to a large geographic region of Russia and Asia known for its long and severe winters.

Terrific Tigers

Siberian tigers have distinctive orange, black, and white fur that makes them stand out. They are awe-inspiring when seen in their natural habitat for which they were named: the snowy forests and **taiga** of the Siberian region of eastern Russia and northeastern China.

All One Species

The Siberian tiger is also known by other names, such as the continental tiger and the Amur tiger. Recently, scientists **categorized** all tigers on mainland Asia as Siberian tigers. This includes those formerly known as Bengal, Malayan, Indochinese, South China, and Caspian tigers. The other tiger **species** is the Sumatran tiger. It lives in tropical rain forests and is smaller than the Siberian tiger.

Chapter 1

What Do They Look Like?

All cats look somewhat alike. They have four legs, paws, a tail, and fur. But they differ by species and subspecies, behavior, and **habitat**.

Mammals

Siberian tigers are mammals. All mammals share some things in common. These are called characteristics. Mammals keep a constant body temperature, even as their environment gets warmer or colder. Hair or fur covers their skin. Females give birth to live young and feed them with milk that the mother produces.

Siberian, or Amur, tigers are also sometimes called Manchurian tigers, Ussurian tigers, and Korean tigers.

Giant Tigers

Massive in size, male Siberian tigers weigh about 500 pounds (227 kg). That's as much as two refrigerators. Some are even larger, although females are smaller than males. From head to tail, these tigers grow to about 10 feet (3 m) long. That's bigger than a king-sized bed!

Subwhat?

Animals within a species group can reproduce offspring that are fertile, or able to have babies. Subspecies is a term that refers to animals of a species that live in different areas and differ in size or have physical differences such as shape.

Fur Coats

Like other mammals, tigers are covered with fur. They're known for their orange body fur with blackish stripes. Siberian tigers' chests and stomachs, as well as portions of their faces, are white. Their fur is thick—the thickest of all tigers. This is especially true in the winter. The thick fur on their underbelly protects them when they are lying on snow and cold ground.

Siberian tigers have longer hair on the back of their heads and, in winter, an extra layer of fat on their bellies and flanks. This helps keep them warm in very cold environments.

No two tigers have the same stripe pattern. They vary in length and color. Their coats are also brighter in summer.

Stripes for Camo

Each Siberian tiger has unique stripes. These stripes exist on the animal's skin and its fur. Scientists think the striped patterns provide **camouflage** for Siberian tigers when they're in forests. Some of their **prey** cannot distinguish between shades of red and green, so a tiger's stripes help it to blend into forest and grassland environments.

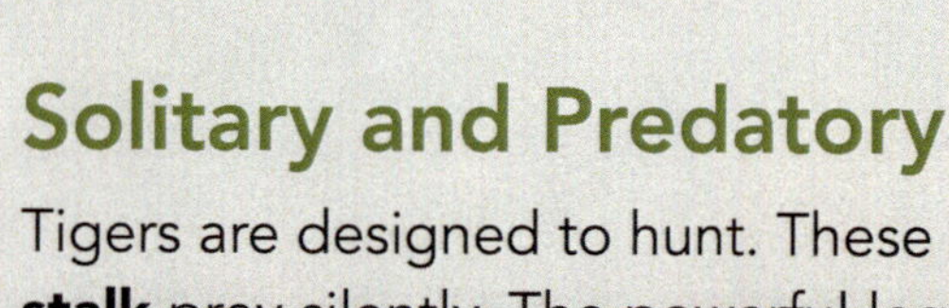

Solitary and Predatory

Tigers are designed to hunt. These beasts walk and **stalk** prey silently. The powerful legs of a Siberian tiger help it to launch into the air with a 20-foot (6 m) leap—or longer. Their claws and fangs help them capture prey and tear through meals.

Meat Eaters

Siberian tigers are carnivores, or meat eaters. They can eat up to 66 pounds (30 kg) of meat when hungry, although most meals are 17 to 22 pounds (8–10 kg) at a time.

Tigers need teeth for survival. They don't chew their food, but shear chunks from their prey's body. As they age, tigers often lose teeth, making them more likely to starve and die.

Chomping Down

When on a hunt, Siberian tigers stalk quietly. They hunt at night and kill their prey with a bite to the neck or throat. Their curved canine teeth can measure up to 3 inches (7.6 cm) long. They use them to chomp, grip, and carry. Siberian tigers are patient hunters, and sometimes stalk prey for hours. These tigers have large territories, which they mark as their own with urine, or pee.

Tiger Teeth

Like many mammals, tigers are born toothless. Their milk teeth erupt in the first weeks of their lives and they have a full set within a few months. Siberian tigers have 30 adult teeth—four canine teeth, 12 incisors, 12 premolars, and two molars. Their canines are strong and allow them to chomp and hold onto prey. Premolars and molars allow them to tear through flesh so they can eat and swallow.

Chapter 2

Home and Habitat

In the wild, Siberian tigers are native to South and Central Asia. Many now roam the birch tree forests of eastern Russia.

Then and Now

Today, most wild Siberian tigers live in the woodlands in Far East Russia in regions called Primorsky Krai and Khabarovsk Krai. Krai means edge or frontier in Russian. A small number of around 10 lives in northeastern China. It is believed that some still live in North Korea. Their habitat used to include much of the Korean Peninsula through northeastern China, and eastern Siberia to Mongolia. Changes in climate, wars, and **poaching** changed that.

In the Wild

An estimated 265 to 486 Siberian tigers live in the wild, according to the International Union for Conservation of Nature (IUCN). The IUCN takes an inventory of the **conservation** status, or how well an animal or plant is surviving. The IUCN makes a report on species at risk, called the IUCN Red List. The Red List also gives scientific information on how a species can be conserved.

The Sikhote-Alin Nature Reserve is part of a UNESCO World Heritage Site. It protects **endangered** Siberian tigers. Hunting and fishing are forbidden, or not allowed, in the reserve.

The Numbers

The IUCN Red List estimates the main population of wild Siberian tigers lives in Russia's far eastern Sikhote-Alin mountain range. These numbers have increased over the past 80 years. This is due to Russia banning tiger hunting and restricting, or better managing, the hunting of the tiger's main food sources: boar and deer.

Climate Preference

The climate in Siberian tiger territory is cold and harsh. Temperatures can dip to –40 °Fahrenheit (–40 °C) or lower. Snow covers the ground for eight months of the year. The Siberian tiger has more than 1 inch (2.5 cm) of fat to **insulate** its body in the winter. These magnificent cats are built for winter weather in other ways too. A Siberian tiger's fur gets thicker in the winter. Its coat grows long to prepare for the bitterly cold weather. Its white chest and stomach camouflage with the snow. The rest of its coat becomes paler in the winter to blend in with the snowy environment too.

Real Paw Patrol

The fur on Siberian tigers' paws grows extra thick to keep them warm. In their snowy environment, their wide feet work like snowshoes to distribute their weight over more area. This allows the Siberian tiger to walk across the top of snow instead of sinking into it. A fully grown adult male's front paws can measure 6 to 8 inches (15 to 20 cm) wide.

The Claw

The Siberian tiger's **retractable** claws help them climb trees and mark their territory. They also use their sharp claws as weapons against threats, and to grab and hold prey.

Chapter 3

What to Eat?

Siberian tigers have healthy appetites. They can spend days hunting and stalking prey, sometimes over hundreds of miles. Once they pounce and kill, they tear their prey apart and feast.

On the Menu

Siberian tigers roam through their forest habitats looking for food. Not many large animals live in their icy habitat. Some research shows Siberian tigers can travel more than 600 miles (965 km) while hunting. They mostly prey on large animals such as wild boar, sika, or spotted deer, and small deer called roe deer. They also eat small prey such as rabbits, rodent-like animals called pikas, and salmon from rivers and streams.

The Siberian tiger has excellent eyesight and sensitive whiskers. These help them see and feel movement in the dark.

Siberian tigers have the largest teeth of all living carnivorous land mammals.

Night Hunters

Siberian tigers are nocturnal, or active at night. They rest and play during the day. They often begin to stalk their prey at dusk. It can take a while before a tiger pounces, as they want to get as close as possible without scaring the prey away. Only one in 20 tiger attacks results in a kill. This means that when they are successful, Siberian tigers eat as much as they can. They drag their dead prey to secluded areas where they can take their time eating.

Meal Times

Siberian tigers kill prey about once a week. Summer hunting lands smaller animals—averaging about 17 pounds (8 kg) each. In the winter, they tend to hunt larger animals. They need an average of 22 pounds (10 kg) of food a day, but they can consume three times as much with their huge appetites. Since they don't know how soon they will eat again, Siberian tigers can eat 60 pounds (27 kg) of meat in a single sitting.

Eurasian Wolf

Though they don't prey on each other as food, Eurasian wolves often scavenge from tiger kills. Siberian tigers try to chase the wolves away, which can lead to deadly fights. Often the tiger wins because it is the **apex predator**. Sometimes, wolves manage to kill tiger cubs.

Competitors

As hunters, Siberian tigers eat an all-meat diet. They are the largest cat in the world and the third-largest land carnivore. They have big appetites, but they aren't the only predator in their habitat. Siberian tigers compete with other predator-hunters for food. They share their territory with the Eurasian wolf. Competition can be intense between these two.

In Captivity

Many Siberian tigers live in **captivity**—an estimated 650 to 1,000, which is more than the wild population. Most of these cats are in public zoos and conservation centers. Some zoos have **breeding** programs to help boost the numbers and prevent **extinction**. Ethical breeding programs follow a Species Survival Plan (SSP) to prevent **inbreeding** and ensure **genetic** diversity. About 50 zoos in North America use SSP programs to increase their tiger numbers.

Ethical Breeding

Ethical breeding means looking after the long-term health and impacts on an animal and species. Breeders study the health of the animal. They do genetic testing to ensure the animals they are breeding do not have **hereditary** issues or disorders that would make it difficult for them to survive in the wild. They also limit the number of times a female tiger can be bred.

About 50 North American zoos have Siberian tiger breeding programs, with an estimated 250 tigers. Breeding is for conservation and to ensure a healthy population.

Siberian Tiger Introduction Project

Wildlife conservationists from the Wildlife Conservation Society (WCS) began working with wild Siberian tigers in their Far East Russia habitats in the 1990s. The WCS is a New York-based conservation organization that connects research and zoo breeding. Their goal is to help encourage the survival of Siberian tigers by conserving their environment. They use radio-tracking collars to collect information about where Siberian tigers are in the wild. The WCS hopes to use this research information to introduce Siberian tigers to traditional habitats as well as areas where other tigers once ranged.

Chapter 4

Siberian Tiger Behavior

Siberian tigers are considered solitary and territorial animals. Unless they are raising young or **mating**, they tend to live alone. They mark their scent on trees to keep other tigers away—they don't want competition in their territory.

Siberian tigers must cover great distances to find prey they want to eat. They stalk an animal until they are close enough to pounce.

Roaming the Range

With huge hunting territories, or ranges, Siberian tigers typically cover about 6 miles (10 km) every day. But they can roam for up to 25 miles (40 km) in a single day. They can be fast too—racing at 45 miles per hour (72 kph) when chasing prey. Wild tigers need large areas of land to roam on.

Strong and Smart

Siberian tigers save their energy for hunts. They can cover a lot of territory in a day. Like most big cats, Siberian tigers can also leap great lengths. A single jump can be more than 20 feet (6 m) in length and 16 feet (5 m) high. Long leaps can tire a tiger, so they only do it for a short period of time.

Sleepy Tigers

Siberian tigers rest during much of the day—and evening. In fact, they can spend from 15 to 20 hours a day dozing. Sleep is important for conserving energy. It also helps their bodies and brains function and recover from hunting, stalking, and patrolling their territory. Being nocturnal has its advantages. Tigers are less likely to have direct encounters with humans at night, which means fewer threats from poachers.

Sometimes if hunting is unsuccessful, a tired tiger may lie down to rest instead of continuing to chase their prey.

Small Cat, Big Cat

Tigers are not house cats, but they share some behaviors with domestic cats. House cats share 95.6 percent of their genetic makeup with tigers. Both are carnivores who rely on their **instincts** to hunt. They stalk, pounce, and play. Play is often used to teach young how to hunt. But there is also a great deal of difference between house cats and tigers. Siberian tigers are wild animals, even in captivity. Their natural instincts are strong. Their primary instinct is survival and they use all of their senses for this. They teach their offspring to survive. One example of this is how mother tigers teach their young to hunt.

Instinct

Even in captivity, Siberian tigers can be dangerous. These big cats are fed by their trainers and do not need to hunt. But they will not hesitate to attack a stranger in their enclosures. It is a natural reaction to real and **perceived** threats.

Purrty Good Imitation

Siberian tigers are unable to purr. Instead, they make a sound called a "chuff" when they are content. It sounds like a ruffled snort. Chuffing is just one way tigers vocally communicate. They also growl, roar, and moan. Tigers roar loudly to let other animals know they are in their territory and to attract a mate.

When Siberian tigers feel threatened they hiss—which is nearly a growl. Their moans sound like a cow's deep moo or a house cat's meow.

Tigers have eyelids and lashes, but like alligators and crocodiles, they also have a membrane on each eye that removes dust and helps keep their eyes moist.

Tiger's Eye

Like many mammals, including **primates**, Siberian tigers have eyes on the front of their heads. This gives them what is called binocular vision. Binocular vision allows the two eyes to work together, with each eye seeing from different angles. The brain then perceives the view from the two eyes as one.

Night Vision

Binocular vision gives Siberian tigers good **depth perception**. This means they can accurately judge distance. Tigers also have excellent night vision. They can see six times better at night than humans. A structure at the back of their eye, called the tapetum lucidum, reflects light and makes their eyes glow at night when light is shone on them.

Smell Me Later

Although Siberian tigers live alone, they do communicate with other animals, including other tigers, in a number of ways. They use scent as a marker. Scent glands on their tails, paws, and faces leave behind each tiger's specific "mark" or scent. They also spray urine to leave scent messages called **pheromones** for other tigers. They mark trees with their scent to keep other tigers out of their territory.

A tiger's whiskers are part of its sense of touch. There are five different types. The whiskers on a tiger's face measure about 6 inches (15 cm) long.
There are also whiskers on random parts of the body. These are called tylotrich whiskers.
Whiskers located above the eyes are called superciliary.
Tigers can hear high-pitched sounds and movements. The ears themselves can move to locate a sound.
Mystacial whiskers are on the tiger's snout and are used to find their way in the dark and to attack prey. Cheek whiskers are set behind the mystacial whiskers.
On the back of a tiger's front legs there are carpal whiskers.

Chapter 5

The Next Generation

In the wild, Siberian tigers don't have a "mating season." They can mate at any time of year, but mating usually occurs during the long, cold winter months from November through April. Mating also depends on when a female is ready.

Sending a Message

When a female Siberian tiger is in estrus, or ready to mate, she attracts a male by scratching trees and leaving "friendly" urine deposits on them. This allows the male to smell her scent messages, or pheromones. The female may also vocalize or call out to attract a male. When they meet, the male and female tiger spend five or six days together. They usually circle each other and vocalize before mating repeatedly.

Female Siberian tigers outnumber males—two to four females to one male—by adulthood.

Siberian tigers usually begin to mate between the ages of three to five years.

Mating and Pregnancy

Mating can take place over several days. After mating, the two part. Gestation, or the length of pregnancy, is about three to three and a half months. In the final days of her pregnancy, the female tiger searches for a safe place to have her litter of cubs. She wants to hide her baby tigers. Most litters are two to four cubs, but they can be as large as seven.

Protecting Cubs

The mother is protective of her newborn Siberian tiger cubs. If she feels threatened, she moves them to a different den. A mother tiger only leaves her cubs when it is necessary to drink and hunt for food. She must take care of herself because she needs to eat a lot more food to have good milk supply for her cubs. Scientists estimate nursing mother tigers need to eat 50 percent more food than usual to maintain their energy with the nursing demands of their cubs.

Tiger cubs weigh about 1.75 to 3.5 pounds (0.8–1.6 kg) at birth, but quickly gain weight.

Nursing Young

Newborn tiger cubs are completely helpless and dependent on their mother. They're born blind with their eyes closed, and only open their eyes when they're about a week old. Their vision begins to develop after several weeks. Mothers spend about 70 percent of their time nursing. That decreases as the cubs grow older. Cubs also grow fast. By the time they are three months old, mothers spend about 30 percent of their day nursing.

Mother tigers groom and lick their young. This helps the cub's blood to circulate and their bowels to work properly.

Tiger cubs are often ready to leave their den to explore by the time they are around two months old.

Little Carnivores

Around two months of age, tiger cubs begin to eat solid food from prey the mother provides. When cubs are about four months old, they begin to play, pounce, and wrestle with siblings. This play provides tiger cubs with skills they will use all of their lives as hunters. Cubs often stop nursing by six months—but they still depend on the prey that their mother hunts and brings to them.

Male tiger cubs weigh between 90 and 110 pounds (41–50 kg) at six months—or about the weight of a fully grown male Great Pyrenees dog. Females weigh about 60 to 95 pounds (27–43 kg)—or about the weight of a fully grown female rottweiler dog.

Socialization

Siberian tiger cubs begin following their mother out of their dens, or rearing areas, at about two months of age. They play with each other and learn survival skills. Cubs begin to hunt along with their mother at about eight to 10 months old. Some behavior is instinctual, but mothers teach their cubs how to fend for themselves. They learn to hunt by hunting. They build muscle memory and strength as they grow and age.

Play is an important part of learning to be a tiger. Siberian tiger siblings fight and pounce in preparation for a life on their own.

On Their Own

By the time a Siberian tiger is two to two and a half years old, it can be independent. Sometimes females stay longer with their mother, but young male tigers travel through the forests by themselves. Young tigers tend to establish territories close to their mother's range. Most Siberian tigers live to be about 15 years old.

Chapter 6

Siberian Tiger Conservation

Siberian tigers are apex predators. This means they are a predator at the top of the food chain with no natural predators. However, they struggle to survive in their wild environment. Humans and human activities are the greatest threat to them—and to all tigers.

Dwindling Habitat

Siberian tigers are particularly at risk due to their habitat and already low populations. As Siberian tigers lose their forest habitats to **deforestation**, their ranges become limited, and they have fewer prey to hunt.

Extinction is irreversible. Once the last of a species dies, they cannot be replaced.

Shrinking Gene Pool

When forests shrink or are destroyed by human activities such as logging, tigers are cut off from their homes and food. Their ranges change and it becomes more difficult to find a wider group for mating. This changes the gene pool, or the number of tigers able to mate and have babies. In addition, fewer den sites are available for young cubs, leaving them vulnerable to predators.

Poaching Tigers

Poaching is the illegal selling or killing of wildlife. It's a big problem for the Siberian tiger population in the wild. Their **pelts**, claws, and teeth are often sold illegally, sometimes for use in traditional medicines. Poachers also illegally kill or capture the animals that tigers eat. This leaves tigers hungry.

Disease

Chronic hunger weakens a tiger's immune system, making them more vulnerable to diseases. Outbreaks of Canine Distemper Virus (CDV) make Siberian tigers even less able to hunt. This **contagious** virus can damage their brains, nervous systems, and lungs. The Wildlife Conservation Society (WCS) is studying ways to detect CDV in Russia by mapping the location of tigers with the virus and helping veterinarians provide treatment. WCS hopes to broaden conservation and prevent future outbreaks of the deadly disease.

Wildlife conservation groups have developed mobile field test kits for CDV for biologists working in the field. These are briefcase-sized kits that can be used in remote regions of the world for quick disease testing.

Protecting Habitat

Protecting the Siberian tiger's habitat has helped stop some poaching, as have laws in many countries that prevent the importing and selling of tiger parts. Some wildlife conservation organizations have taken an active approach to building populations. Siberian tigers are scheduled to be introduced in a national park in the country of Kazakhstan. The park is where Caspian tigers, their close cousins, once roamed. Caspian tigers were considered extinct in 1948. They once ranged a vast region that stretched from Türkiye to China. Most were killed off by sport hunters, humans taking over their habitat, and disease.

Endangered Species

Currently, scientists consider Siberian tigers an endangered species. Without conservation efforts it is likely they will no longer exist in the near future. They are on the IUCN's Red List. That means this tiger faces high risks of extinction in the wild based on the threats they face for survival. There are different levels of endangerment. In the past, Siberian tigers were critically endangered, with only 50 living in the wild. Conservation efforts have helped restore their population, although there are still fewer than 500 living in the wild today.

Conservation efforts such as the California Condor Recovery Program helped bring the condor from endangered species to threatened species. By 1982, there were 22 condors in the wild. Today there are more than 300.

Scientific Measures for Survival

Scientists evaluate a lot of research and data to decide if an animal species needs help to survive. They look at:

- total population, and if the population is growing or decreasing
- natural habitat availability and how much habitat is needed
- conservation efforts

Based on their findings, biologists know Siberian tigers are in trouble.

Apex predators **cull** herds of the easiest-to-catch prey, such as the oldest or weakest. These animals might be more likely to catch and spread disease to the herd.

Ecosystem Balance

The loss of an apex predator alters an entire food chain, or the links between all living things in a specific environment. If an apex predator dies out, it can cause an overpopulation of herbivores, or prey species. With nothing keeping their populations in check, **ecosystems** can be harmed through overgrazing and plant destruction. This can also weaken the natural growth of forests and lead to more forest fires.

Conservation Helps

Conservation and research over the last 30 years have helped preserve and protect the Siberian tiger's habitat. The cold-climate taiga, or snow forests that are their home in the wild, is the world's largest land biome. There is so much more to learn about this geographical region and the animals that live there. Siberian tiger conservation through zoo programs and wildland protection efforts have helped these big cats survive. But more needs to be done to ensure they can thrive long-term in the wild.

Although hunting is limited by national governments today, it still happens. Often, conservation requires a multi-country effort. Many communities are involved also, as people who live closest to the wild animals are more likely to have interactions and knowledge about them.

apex predator (EY-peks PRED-uh-ter): A predator with no natural predators of its own

breeding (BREE-ding): Producing offspring

camouflage (KAM-uh-flahzh): Colors and patterns that help an animal blend in with its natural surroundings

captivity (kap-TIV-i-tee): When an animal lives under human control or care

categorized (KAT-i-guh-rahyzd): Put into a group of similar things

conservation (kon-ser-VEY-shuhn): The protection of animals, plants, and their habitats

contagious (kuhn-TEY-juhs): Able to be spread from one person or animal to another

cull (kuhl): To choose or select from a group

deforestation (dee-fawr-uh-STEY-shuhn): The permanent clearing of forests or large areas of trees

depth perception (depth per-SEP-shuhn): The ability to see objects in three dimensions and judge how far away they are

ecosystems (EE-koh-sis-tuhms): Communities of living and nonliving things in their environments

endangered (en-DEYN-jerd): An animal or plant species that is considered to be at a very high risk of becoming extinct in the wild

extinction (ik-STINGK-shuhn): When an animal or plant species completely dies out and disappears from Earth forever

feline (FEE-lahyn): Of or relating to the cat family

genetic (juh-NET-ik): Relating to the study of how certain features are passed from parents to their offspring

habitat (HAB-i-tat): The place where an animal or plant naturally lives and grows

hereditary (huh-RED-i-ter-ee): Passed from parent to offspring before birth

inbreeding (IN-bree-ding): When closely related plants or animals produce offspring together

instinct (IN-stingkt): Natural behavior that an animal is born knowing and that is not taught

insulate (IN-suh-leyt): To protect something from cold or heat

mating (MEY-ting): When a male and female animal join together for the purpose of producing offspring

pelt (pelt): The skin of a dead animal with its hair or fur still attached

perceived (per-SEEVD): Sensed something by instinct but not necessarily fact

pheromone (FER-uh-mohn): A chemical substance that an animal produces to communicate with other animals of the same species

poach (pohch): To catch or kill an animal illegally

prey (prey): Animals that are hunted and eaten by other animals

primates (PRAHY-meyts): A group of mammals that includes people, apes, and monkeys

retractable (ri-TRAKT-uh-buhl): Able to be pulled back or in

species (SPEE-sheez): A group of living things that are very similar and can have babies together

stalk (stawk): To follow prey carefully and quietly while hunting

taiga (TAHY-guh): A forest of the cold subarctic region that lies just south of the Arctic Circle

INDEX

COMPREHENSION QUESTIONS

1. True or False: All Siberian tigers have the same pattern of stripes.

2. Siberian tigers kill prey about ________ a week.
   a. once
   b. twice
   c. five times

3. True or False: Siberian tigers hunt their prey during the day.

4. Siberian tigers have ______ adult teeth.
   a. 18
   b. 30
   c. 48

5. True or False: Siberian tigers do not purr.

6. A Siberian tiger's whiskers are part of its sense of ______________.
   a. smell
   b. taste
   c. touch

7. True or False: Scientists consider Siberian tigers an endangered species.

8. Most Siberian tigers live to be about _______ years old.
   a. 5
   b. 10
   c. 15

ANSWERS
1. False, 2. a, 3. False, 4. b, 5. True,
6. c, 7. True, 8. c

About the Author

Annette Whipple is the author of many children's books, including *The Laura Ingalls Wilder Companion: A Chapter-by-Chapter Guide, Whooo Knew? The Truth About Owls, and Quirky Critter Devotions: 52 Wild Wonders for Kids.* When Annette's not reading or writing, you might find her baking for her family in Pennsylvania. Get to know her at AnnetteWhipple.com.

Written by: Annette Whipple

Editor: Ellen Rodger

Proofreader: Melissa Boyce

Design and layout: Tammy McGarr

Production manager: Candice Campbell

Image Credits

Shutterstock: goran_safarek p 41 (bottom), Denis Kabelev p 41 (top left)

Wikimedia Commons: Creative Commons p 12 (map), 20,
p 43 (middle); Public Domain, p 39

All other images from Shutterstock

Crabtree Publishing

crabtreebooks.com **800-387-7650**

Hardcover	978-1-0398-8077-1
Paperback	978-1-0398-8438-0
Ebook (pdf)	978-1-0398-8197-6
Epub	978-1-0398-8317-8

Published in Canada
Crabtree Publishing
616 Welland Avenue
St. Catharines, Ontario
L2M 5V6

Published in the United States
Crabtree Publishing
347 Fifth Avenue
Suite 1402-145
New York, New York, 10016

Library and Archives Canada Cataloguing in Publication
Available at Library and Archives Canada

Library of Congress Cataloging-in-Publication Data
Available at the Library of Congress

Printed in the U.S.A./CP022026